CW00592019

RIVER SONGS

Selections from the Psalms with prayer meditations

Photo:	Page
Stockphotos international:	Front cover, 30-31 52-53,72-73
Robert C. Hayes:	4-5, 22, 63, 65, 68
Urpo A. Tarnanen:	6-7, 10-11, 14-15, 26, 27, 36, 37
	44, 45, 62, 69, 76, 77, 78-79
Explorer:	8-9
Joachim Kinkelin:	12-13, 34-35
G. Grønbeck:	16
Photo Solbjerghøj:	17
Bavaria:	18-19
Alan Bedding:	20-21
R. Rauth:	23, 42-43, 50-51, 70-71-
Wilfred Konrad:	24-25
Otto Wikkelsø:	28
Tony Stone Ass.:	29, 32-33, 54-55, 64
Willy P. Burkhardt:	38-39
Scandinavia:	40, 41, 46, 47, 49, 58-59
	66-67
Peter Østergrens:	48
G + M Kohler:	56
Bildarchiv Huber:	57
Löbl - Schreyer:	60-61
Zefa:	74-75
Walter Geiersperger:	80

© Copyright Scandinavia Publishing House
Nørregade 32
DK 1165 Copenhagen K
Denmark
Tel. 01-140091

© Text: Ben Alex

Printed in Hong Kong by C & C Offset Printing Co., Ltd.

ISBN 87 87732 61 0

RIVER SONGS

Selections from the Psalms with prayer meditations

Text by Ben Alex

Scandinavia

*He split the
rocks in the desert and
gave them water as abundant
as the seas; he brought streams out
of a rocky crag and made water
flow down like
rivers.*

But I pray to you, O Lord,
in the time of your favor; in your great
love, O God, answer me with your sure salvation.
Rescue me from the mire, do not let me sink; deliver
me from those who hate me, from the deep waters. Do not
let the floodwaters engulf me or the depths swallow me
up or the pit close its mouth over me. Answer me, O Lord,
out of the goodness of your love; in your great mercy turn
to me. Do not hide your face from your servant;
answer me quickly, for I am in trouble.
Come near and rescue me; redeem
me because of my foes.

Psalm 68

A father to the fatherless

Sing to God, sing praise to his name, extol him who rides on the clouds – his name is the Lord– and rejoice before him.

May God arise, may his enemies be scattered; may his foes flee before him.
As smoke is blown away by the wind, may you blow them away; as wax melts before the fire, may the wicked perish before God.
But may the righteous be glad and rejoice before God; may they be happy and joyful.

Sing to God, sing praise to his name, extol him who rides on the clouds – his name is the Lord– and rejoice before him.
A father to the fatherless, a defender of widows, is God in his holy dwelling.
God sets the lonely in families, he leads forth the prisoners with singing; but the rebellious live in a sun-scorched land.

So high mounts Your splendour,
so low drops Your mercy
that no one;
from greatest to smallest,
can reach to Your knees
nor stoop to Your feet.

God reigns from high places

The earth shook, The heavens poured down rain, before God, the One of Sinai, before God, the God of Israel.

When you went out before your people, O God, when you marched through the wasteland, *Selah*, the earth shook, the heavens poured down rain, before God, the One of Sinai, before God, the God of Israel.
You gave abundant showers, O God; you refreshed your weary inheritance.
Your people settled in it, and from your bounty, O God, you provided for the poor.

The Lord announced the word, and great was the company of those who proclaimed it: "Kings and armies flee in haste; in the camps men divide the plunder.
Even while you sleep among the campfires, the wings of my dove are sheathed with silver, its feathers with shining gold."
When the Almighty scattered the kings in the land, it was like snow fallen on Zalmon.

The mountains of Bashan are majestic mountains; rugged are the mountains of Bashan.
Why gaze in envy, O rugged mountains, at the mountain where God chooses to reign, where the Lord himself will dwell forever?
The chariots of God are tens of thousands and thousands of thousands; the Lord has come from Sinai into his sanctuary.
When you ascended on high, you led captives in your train; you received gifts from men, even from the rebellious– that you, O Lord God, might dwell there.

Praise be to the Lord, to God our Savior, who daily bears our burdens.

You led us to a land of promise
where we did not strive
to make our vineyards blossom,
but You
warmed the seeds from below
and gave showers of rain from above.

Proclaim the power of God

*Our God is a God who saves; from the Sovereign Lord comes
escape from death.*
*Surely God will crush the heads of his enemies, the hairy
crowns of those who go on in their sins.*
*The Lord says, "I will bring you from Bashan; I will bring
you from the depths of the sea, that you may plunge your feet
in the blood of your foes, while the tongues of your dogs have
their share."*

Your procession has come into view, O God, the procession
of my God and King into the sanctuary.
In front are the singers, after them the musicians; with them
are the maidens playing tambourines.
Praise God in the great congregation; praise the Lord in the
assembly of Israel.
There is the little tribe of Benjamin, leading them, there the
great throng of Judah's princes, and there the princes of
Zebulun and of Naphtali.

Summon your power, O God, show us your strength, O God,
as you have done before.
Because of your temple at Jerusalem kings will bring you
gifts.
Rebuke the beast among the reeds, the herd of bulls among
the calves of the nations. Humbled, may it bring bars of silver.
Scatter the nations who delight in war.
Envoys will come from Egypt; Cush will submit herself to
God.
Sing to God, O kingdoms of the earth, sing praise to the Lord,
Selah, to him who rides the ancient skies above, who thunders
with mighty voice.
Proclaim the power of God, whose majesty is over Israel,
whose power is in the skies.
You are awesome, O God, in your sanctuary; the God of
Israel gives power and strength to his people. Praise be to
God!

I love to enter Your house
with thanksgiving and in unity
with Your redeemed people;
You descend from Your place and
inhabit Your people with presence
and power. Your trail fills the temple.

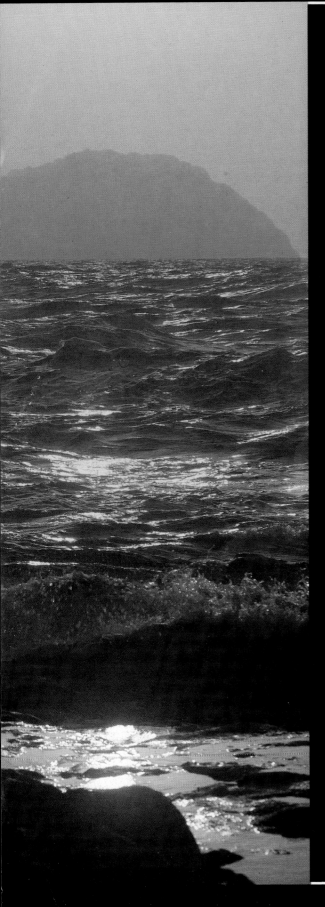

Save me, O God

But I pray to you, O Lord, in the time of your favor; in your great love, O God, answer me with your sure salvation.

Save me, O God, for the waters have come up to my neck. I sink in the miry depths, where there is no foothold. I have come into the deep waters; the floods engulf me.
I am worn out calling for help; my throat is parched. My eyes fail, looking for my God.
Those who hate me without reason outnumber the hairs of my head; many are my enemies without cause, those who seek to destroy me. I am forced to restore what I did not steal.
You know my folly, O God; my guilt is not hidden from you.

May those who hope in you not be disgraced because of me, O Lord, the Lord Almighty; may those who seek you not be put to shame because of me, O God of Israel.
For I endure scorn for your sake, and shame covers my face.
I am a stranger to my brothers, an alien to my own mother's sons; for zeal for your house consumes me, and the insults of those who insult you fall on me.
When I weep and fast, I must endure scorn; when I put on sackcloth, people make sport of me.
Those who sit at the gate mock me, and I am the song of the drunkards.

But I pray to you, O Lord, in the time of your favor; in your great love, O God, answer me with your sure salvation.

When I feel the closest to You,
when I think I hear your voice;
suddenly you are not there.
The ocean seems so big and the horizon
scatters into a thousand pieces.
You are a God who hides himself
until the moment I despair.
There Your presence comes gently
and quietly, in an ordinary moment.

Come near and rescue me

Rescue me from the mire, do not let me sink; deliver me from those who hate me, from the deep waters. Do not let the floodwaters engulf me or the depths swallow me up or the pit close its mouth over me. Answer me, O Lord, out of the goodness of your love; in your great mercy turn to me. Do not hide your face from your servant; answer me quickly, for I am in trouble. Come near and rescue me; redeem me because of my foes.

You know how I am scorned, disgraced and shamed; all my enemies are before you. Scorn has broken my heart and has left me helpless; I looked for sympathy, but there was none, for comforters, but I found none. They put gall in my food and gave me vinegar for my thirst.

May the table set before them become a snare; may it become retribution and a trap. May their eyes be darkened so they cannot see, and their backs be bent forever. Pour out your wrath on them; let your fierce anger overtake them. May their place be deserted; let there be no one to dwell in their tents. For they persecute those you wound and talk about the pain of those you hurt. Charge them with crime upon crime; do not let them share in your salvation. May they be blotted out of the book of life and not be listed with the righteous.

I am in pain and distress; may your salvation, O God, protect me.

I will praise God's name in song and glorify him with thanksgiving. This will please the Lord more than an ox, more than a bull with its horns and hoofs. The poor will see and be glad– you who seek God, may your hearts live! The Lord hears the needy and does not despise his captive people.

Let heaven and earth praise him, the seas and all that move in them, for God will save Zion and rebuild the cities of Judah. Then people will settle there and possess it; the children of his servants will inherit it, and those who love his name will dwell there.

When I feel lonely and let down,
confused and misunderstood,
help me to see that You use
circumstance and people
for Your purpose.
It all comes from Your mighty hand
and is, therefore,
the redeeming force in my life.

You are my deliverer

Yet I am poor and needy; come quickly to me, O God.
You are my help and my deliverer; O Lord, do not delay.

Hasten, O God, to save me; O Lord, come quickly to help me.
May those who seek my life be put to shame and confusion;
may all who desire my ruin be turned back in disgrace.
May those who say to me, "Aha! Aha!" turn back because of
their shame.
But may all who seek you rejoice and be glad in you; may
those who love your salvation always say, "Let God be
exalted!"

Yet I am poor and needy; come quickly to me, O God. You
are my help and my deliverer; O Lord, do not delay.

Why do my eyes seek the darkness
when there is still light around?
Why does it take so much praise
to outweigh the criticism?
Why so many friends
to outnumber one enemy?
In the difficult times
when my praise of You does not come easily,
I shall turn to Your people,
see You in their midst,
and say, "Let God Be Exalted!"

Psalm 71

My confidence since my youth

Be my rock of refuge, to which I can always go; give the command to save me, for you are my rock and my fortress.

In you, O Lord, I have taken refuge; let me never be put to shame.
Rescue me and deliver me in your righteousness; turn your ear to me and save me.
Be my rock of refuge, to which I can always go; give the command to save me, for you are my rock and my fortress.
Deliver me, O my God, from the hand of the wicked, from the grasp of evil and cruel men.

For you have been my hope, O Sovereign Lord, my confidence since my youth.
From birth I have relied on you; you brought me forth from my mother's womb. I will ever praise you.
I have become like a portent to many, but you are my strong refuge.
My mouth is filled with your praise, declaring your splendor all day long.

Do not cast me away when I am old; do not forsake me when my strength is gone.
For my enemies speak against me; those who wait to kill me conspire together.
They say, "God has forsaken him; pursue him and seize him, for no one will rescue him."
Be not far from me, O God; come quickly, O my God, to help me.
May my accusers perish in shame; may those who want to harm me be covered with scorn and disgrace.

From the days of my youth I relied on You.
Growing old, will You still be my strength?
To grow old in You must be beautifully rich:
a lifetime receiving Your gifts;
full of lessons learned, forgiveness for erring.
A life still ahead: Eternity,
built on a foundation already laid.
To grow old in You: Your Purpose
accomplished in me.

He will rule
from sea to sea and from
the River to the ends of
the earth.

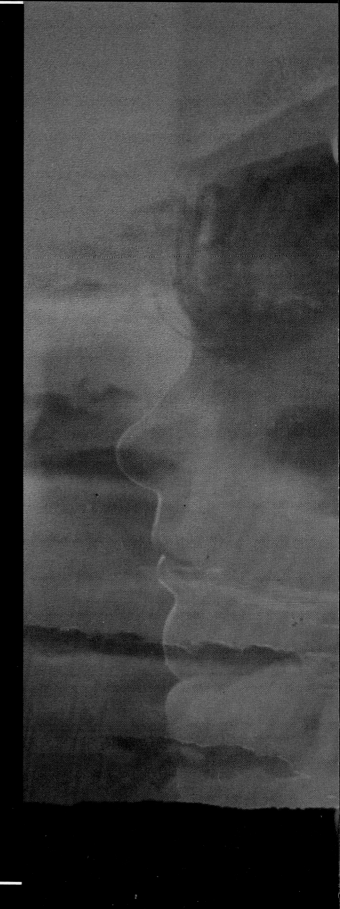

I will ever praise you

Since my youth, O God, you have taught me, and to this day I declare your marvelous deeds.

But as for me, I will always have hope; I will praise you more and more.
My mouth will tell of your righteousness, of your salvation all day long, though I know not its measure.
I will come and proclaim your mighty acts, O Sovereign Lord; I will proclaim your righteousness, yours alone. Since my youth, O God, you have taught me, and to this day I declare your marvelous deeds.
Even when I am old and gray, do not forsake me, O God, till I declare your power to the next generation, your might to all who are to come.

Your righteousness reaches to the skies, O God, you who have done great things. Who, O God, is like you?
Though you have made me see troubles, many and bitter, you will restore my life again; from the depths of the earth you will again bring me up.
You will increase my honor and comfort me once again.

I will praise you with the harp for your faithfulness, O my God; I will sing praise to you with the lyre, O Holy One of Israel.
My lips will shout for joy when I sing praise to you– I, whom you have redeemed.
My tongue will tell of your righteous acts all day long, for those who wanted to harm me have been put to shame and confusion.

In You there's always forgiveness for the past and hope for the future, regardless of the thoughts and feelings that torment me; regardless of my circumstances, bitter though they may be. Life is a circle which will always bring me back to comfort and peace.

Psalm 72

The royal son

*In his days the righteous will flourish; prosperity will abound
till the moon is no more.*

Endow the king with your justice, O God, the royal son with
your righteousness.
He will judge your people in righteousness, your afflicted one
with justice.
The mountains will bring prosperity to the people, the hills the
fruit of righteousness.
He will defend the afflicted among the people and save the
children of the needy; he will crush the oppressor.

He will endure as long as the sun, as long as the moon,
through all generations.
He will be like the rain falling on a mown field, like showers
watering the earth.
In his days the righteous will flourish; prosperity will abound
till the moon is no more.

He will rule from sea to sea and from the River to the ends of
the earth.
The desert tribes will bow before him and his enemies will lick
the dust.
The kings of Tarshish and of distant shores will bring tribute
to him; the kings of Sheba and Seba will present him gifts.
All kings will bow down to him and all nations will serve him.

*Before You I have no demands. Still yet, I
meditate on the promises of Your word,
of the appointed time for every righteous man.
Still yet, I
believe in You for the grace
worked into my life.*

May the earth be filled with his glory

May his name endure forever; may it continue as long as the sun.
All nations will be blessed through him, and they will call him blessed.

For he will deliver the needy who cry out, the afflicted who have no one to help.
He will take pity on the weak and the needy and save the needy from death.
He will rescue them from oppression and violence, for precious is their blood in his sight.

Long may he live! May gold from Sheba be given to him. May people ever pray for him and bless him all day long.
Let grain abound throughout the land; on the tops of the hills may it sway. Let its fruit flourish like Lebanon; let it thrive like the grass of the field.
May his name endure forever; may it continue as long as the sun.

All nations will be blessed through him, and they will call him blessed.
Praise be to the Lord God, the God of Israel, who alone does marvelous deeds.
Praise be to his glorious name for ever; may the whole earth be filled with his glory.
Amen and Amen.

This concludes the prayers of David son of Jesse.

May we bring glory to You
through the fruit of our lives.
We are the golden, swaying wheat.
We are the seeds of a Kingdom to come.
We long to be a part of that world
filled with Your glory O God.

In God's sanctuary

This is what the wicked are like – always carefree, they increase in wealth. Surely in vain have I kept my heart pure; in vain have I washed my hands in innocence.

Surely God is good to Israel, to those who are pure in heart.

But as for me, my feet had almost slipped; I had nearly lost my foothold. For I envied the arrogant when I saw the prosperity of the wicked.

They have no struggles; their bodies are healthy and strong. They are free from the burdens common to man; they are not plagued by human ills. Therefore pride is their necklace; they clothe themselves with violence. From their callous hearts comes iniquity; the evil conceits of their minds know no limits. They scoff, and speak with malice; in their arrogance they threaten oppression. Their mouths lay claim to heaven, and their tongues take possession of the earth. Therefore their people turn to them and drink up waters in abundance. They say, "How can God know? Does the Most High have knowledge?"

This is what the wicked are like– always carefree, they increase in wealth.

Surely in vain have I kept my heart pure; in vain have I washed my hands in innocence. All day long I have been plagued; I have been punished every morning.

If I had said, "I will speak thus," I would have betrayed this generation of your children. When I tried to understand all this, it was oppressive to me till I entered the sanctuary of God; then I understood their final destiny.

Somehow, when I enter Your presence
everything falls into place.
In the world, I am tempted to think
as the world, to take life
into my own hands, and forget
the path of Your Kingdom.
Life is a slippery road.
In Your presence,
I realize the vanity of those
who want to travel on their own.

The strength of my heart

But as for me, it is good to be near God. I have made the
Sovereign Lord my refuge; I will tell of all your deeds.

Surely you place them on slippery ground; you cast them
down to ruin.
How suddenly are they destroyed, completely swept away by
terrors!
As a dream when one awakes, so when you arise, O Lord,
you will despise them as fantasies.

When my heart was grieved and my spirit embittered, I was
senseless and ignorant; I was a brute beast before you.

Yet I am always with you; you hold me by my right hand.
You guide me with your counsel, and afterwards you will take
me into glory.
Whom have I in heaven but you? And being with you, I desire
nothing on earth.
My flesh and my heart may fail, but God is the strength of my
heart and my portion forever.

Those who are far from you will perish; you destroy all who
are unfaithful to you.
But as for me, it is good to be near God. I have made the
Sovereign Lord my refuge; I will tell of all your deeds.

As I walk on with You
I realize the fragility
of the feet once so determined,
of the heart once so strong.
There were things I wanted to accomplish,
dreams I wanted to pursue.
I rest to gather strength for the final journey,
and it strikes me: nothing matters –
except the presence of Your precious Spirit.

Rise against your enemy

Remember the people you purchased of old, the tribe you redeemed as your inheritance – Mount Zion, where you dwelt.

Why have you rejected us forever, O God? Why does your anger smolder against the sheep of your pasture?
Remember the people you purchased of old, the tribe you redeemed as your inheritance– Mount Zion, where you dwelt.

Pick your way through these everlasting ruins, all this destruction the enemy has brought on the sanctuary.
Your foes roared in the place where you met with us; they set up their standards as signs.
They behaved like men wielding axes to cut through a thicket of trees.
They smashed all the carved paneling with their axes and hatchets.
They burned your sanctuary to the ground; they defiled the dwelling place of your Name.
They said in their hearts, "We will crush them completely!"
They burned every place where God was worshiped in the land.
We are given no miraculous signs; no prophets are left and none of us knows how long this will be.
How long will the enemy mock you, O God? Will the foe revile your name forever?
Why do you hold back your hand, your right hand? Take it from the folds of your garment and destroy them!

So often in history
Your church has been left in ruins:
buildings closed; prayer meetings forbidden;
leaders imprisoned; Your Word confiscated;
the lives of Your people broken.
Will the enemy ever learn?
Will he ever understand that You
use him to bring Your Kingdom to fulfillment?
That persecution nurtures the seed of faith?
That revival follows repression?
That out of death
springs New Life, a thousand fold?!

Rise and defend your cause

Do not let the oppressed retreat in disgrace; may the poor and needy praise your name.

But you, O God, are my king from of old; you bring salvation upon the earth.

It was you who split open the sea by your power; you broke the heads of the monster in the waters.

It was you who crushed the heads of Leviathan and gave him as food to the creatures of the desert.

It was you who opened up springs and streams; you dried up the ever flowing rivers.

The day is yours, and yours also the night; you established the sun and moon.

It was you who set all the boundaries of the earth; you made both summer and winter.

Remember how the enemy has mocked you, O Lord, how foolish people have reviled your name.

Do not hand over the life of your dove to wild beasts; do not forget the lives of your afflicted people forever.

Have regard for your covenant, because haunts of violence fill the dark places of the land.

Do not let the oppressed retreat in disgrace; may the poor and needy praise your name.

Rise up, O God, and defend your cause; remember how fools mock you all day long.

Do not ignore the clamor of your adversaries, the uproar of your enemies, which rises continually.

In the midst of turmoil and uproar
there is always a centre of quietness.
In the centuries of history
Your dove has always survived –
in the cleft of the rock;
in the hearts of Your servants,
where peace rules.
Holy Dove, rest
in the cleft of my rocky heart.

*It was you who opened up
springs and streams; you dried up
the ever flowing rivers.*

Praise to God

As for me, I will declare this forever. I will sing praise to the God of Jacob.

We give thanks to you, O God, we give thanks, for your Name is near; men tell of your wonderful deeds.

You say, "I choose the appointed time; it is I who judge uprightly.
When the earth and all its people quake, it is I who hold its pillars firm. *Selah.*
To the arrogant I say, 'Boast no more;' and to the wicked, 'Do not lift up your horns.
Do not lift your horns against heaven; do not speak with outstretched neck.' "

No one from the east or the west or from the desert can exalt a man.
But it is God who judges: He brings one down, he exalts another.
In the hand of the Lord is a cup full of foaming wine mixed with spices; he pours it out, and all the wicked of the earth drink it down to its very dregs.

As for me, I will declare this forever. I will sing praise to the God of Jacob.
I will cut off the horns of all the wicked, but the horns of the righteous will be lifted up.

Thank You Father,
for the simple things in life:
miracles that come quietly;
joy, as the winner; when
innocence thrives; praise
becomes powerful; and
love, durable.
I receive it all from Your hand –
also the difficult times – and know
that no one can boast nor complain.

Psalm 76

Who can stand before God

Make vows to the Lord your God and fulfill them; let all the neighboring lands bring gifts to the One to be feared.

In Judah God is known; his name is great in Israel.
His tent is in Salem, his dwelling place in Zion.
There he broke the flashing arrows, the shields and the swords, the weapons of war. *Selah.*

You are resplendent with light, more majestic than mountains rich with game.
Valiant men lie plundered, they sleep their last sleep; not one of the warriors can lift his hands.
At your rebuke, O God of Jacob, both horse and chariot lie still.
You alone are to be feared. Who can stand before you when you are angry?
From heaven you pronounced judgment, and the land feared and was quiet– when you O God, rose up to judge, to save all the afflicted of the land. *Selah.*
Surely your wrath against men brings you praise, and the survivors of your wrath are restrained.

Make vows to the Lord your God and fulfill them; let all the neighboring lands bring gifts to the One to be feared.
He breaks the spirit of rulers; he is feared by the kings of the earth.

You break the spirit of rulers
and bend the hearts of men.
When You rise to save
the afflicted of the land
Your wrath brings repentance,
Your mercy, salvation.

Your ways, O God

You are the God who performs miracles; you display your power among the peoples. With your mighty arm you redeemed your people, the descendants of Jacob and Joseph. Selah.

I cried out to God for help; I cried out to God to hear me. When I was in distress, I sought the Lord; at night I stretched out untiring hands and my soul refused to be comforted. I remembered you, O God, and I groaned; I mused, and my spirit grew faint. *Selah.*

You kept my eyes from closing; I was too troubled to speak. I thought about the former days, the years of long ago; I remembered my songs in the night. Myheart mused and my spirit inquired: "Will the Lord reject us forever? Will he never show his favor again? Has his unfailing love vanished forever? Has his promise failed for all time? Has God forgotten to be merciful? Has he in anger withheld his compassion?" *Selah.*

Then I thought, "To this I will appeal: the years of the right hand of the Most High." I will remember the deeds of the Lord; yes, I will remember your miracles of long ago. I will meditate on all your works and consider all your mighty deeds. Your ways, O God, are holy. What god is so great as our God? You are the God who performs miracles; you display your power among the peoples. With your mighty arm you redeemed your people, the descendants of Jacob and Joseph. *Selah.*

The waters saw you, O God, the waters saw you and writhed; the very depths were convulsed. The clouds poured down water, the skies resounded with thunder; your arrows flashed back and forth. Your thunder was heard in the whirlwind, your lightning lit up the world; the earth trembled and quaked. Your path led through the sea, your way through the mighty waters, though your footprints were not seen. You led your people like a flock by the hand of Moses and Aaron.

Most of the time I struggle with questions,
but I know You well enough to believe,
that if there are questions,
there will also be answers.
Right now I do not see Your footprints ahead,
but looking back I see
You are still with me.

Tell your children

Then they would put their trust in God and would not forget his deeds but would keep his commands.

O my people, hear my teaching; listen to the words of my mouth.

I will open my mouth in parables, I will utter things hidden from of old– things we have heard and known, things our fathers have told us.

We will not hide them from their children; we will tell the next generation the praiseworthy deeds of the Lord, his power, and the wonders he has done.

He decreed statutes for Jacob and established the law in Israel, which he commanded our forefathers to teach their children, so the next generation would know them, even the children yet to be born, and they in turn would tell their children.

Then they would put their trust in God and would not forget his deeds but would keep his commands.

They would not be like their forefathers– a stubborn and rebellious generation, whose hearts were not loyal to God, whose spirits were not faithful to him.

The men of Ephraim, though armed with bows, turned back on the day of battle; they did not keep God's covenant and refused to live by his law.

They forgot what he had done, the wonders he had shown them.

He did miracles in the sight of their fathers in the land of Egypt, in the region of Zoan.

He divided the sea and led them through; he made the water stand firm like a wall.

He guided them with the cloud by day and with light from the fire all night.

He split the rocks in the desert and gave them water as abundant as the seas; he brought streams out of a rocky crag and made water flow down like rivers.

Help me not to see my life as isolated,
but rather, in relationship to
generations past, and to come.
For Your word is the golden thread
that weaves a tapestry throughout the ages.
It has come to me by way of others,
help me to pass it on
as it was given to me.

Food in the desert

When the Lord heard them, he was very angry; his fire broke out against Jacob, and his wrath rose against Israel, for they did not believe in God or trust in his deliverance.

But they continued to sin against him, rebelling in the desert against the Most High.
They willfully put God to the test by demanding the food they craved.
They spoke against God, saying, "Can God spread a table in the desert?
When he struck the rock, water gushed out, and streams flowed abundantly. But can he also give us food? Can he supply meat for his people?"
When the Lord heard them, he was very angry; his fire broke out against Jacob, and his wrath rose against Israel, for they did not believe in God or trust in his deliverance.
Yet he gave a command to the skies above and opened the doors of the heavens; he rained down manna for the people to eat, he gave them the grain of heaven.
Men ate the bread of angels; he sent them all the food they could eat.
He let loose the east wind from the heavens and led forth the south wind by his power.
He rained meat down on them like dust, flying birds like sand on the seashore.
He made them come down inside their camp, all around their tents.
They ate till they had more than enough, for he had given them what they craved.

You fed me yesterday, yet still I worry;
will Your providence cover tomorrow?
You fed me today, so I took more than my need;
anxious for days to come.
Help me to live for the present moment;
build my security in You!

The sin of the people

*He remembered that they were but flesh, a passing breeze that
does not return.*

But before they turned from the food they craved, even while
it was still in their mouths, God's anger rose against them; he
put to death the sturdiest among them, cutting down the
young men of Israel.
In spite of all this, they kept on sinning; in spite of his
wonders, they did not believe.
So he ended their days in futility and their years in terror.
Whenever God slew them, they would seek him; they eagerly
turned to him again.
They remembered that God was their Rock, that God Most
High was their Redeemer.
But then they would flatter him with their mouths, lying to
him with their tongues; their hearts were not loyal to him, they
were not faithful to his covenant.
Yet he was merciful; he atoned for their iniquities and did not
destroy them. Time after time he restrained his anger and did
not stir up his full wrath.
He remembered that they were but flesh, a passing breeze that
does not return.

*When the pattern of my life
seems full of futile repetitions,
shine on them,
and lend to them your meaning.
I do not ask you to change the patterns,
but to create in me
the fruits of faithfulness.
You see,
the hardest place for a miracle to happen
is in my own heart.*

Psalm 78

The Lord guides his people

But he brought his people out like a flock; he led them like sheep through the desert. He drove out nations before them and allotted their lands to them as an inheritance; he settled the tribes of Israel in their homes.

How often they rebelled against him in the desert and grieved him in the wasteland! Again and again they put God to the test; they vexed the Holy One of Israel. They did not remember his power– the day he redeemed them from the oppressor, the day he displayed his miraculous signs in Egypt, his wonders in the region of Zoan.
He turned their rivers to blood; they could not drink from their streams. He sent swarms of flies that devoured them and frogs that devastated them. He gave their crops to the grasshopper, their produce to the locust. He destroyed their vines with hail and their sycamore-figs with sleet. He gave over their cattle to the hail, their livestock to bolts of lightning. He unleashed against them his hot anger, his wrath, indignation and hostility– a band of destroying angels. He prepared a path for his anger; he did not spare them from death but gave them over to the plague. He struck down all the firstborn of Egypt, the firstfruits of manhood in the tents of Ham.
But he brought his people out like a flock; he led them like sheep through the desert. He guided them safely, so they were unafraid; but the sea engulfed their enemies. Thus he brought them to the border of his holy land, to the hill country his right hand had taken. He drove out nations before them and allotted their lands to them as an inheritance; he settled the tribes of Israel in their homes.

*There is always
an "out", a "through", and an "into",
for Your covenanted people:
we must die before we can be resurrected;
we must suffer in order to capture Divine joy;
and somewhere along the way –
as we realize there is no return –
we are changed
from being a people of darkness
to children of the light.*

*Save me, O God,
for the waters have come up
to my neck. I sink in the miry depths,
where there is no foothold. I have come
into the deep waters; the
floods engulf me.*

The fire of the Lord

He chose David his servant and took him from the sheep pen; from tending the sheep he brought him to be the shepherd of his people Jacob, of Israel his inheritance.

But they put God to the test and rebelled against the Most High; they did not keep his statutes. Like their fathers they were disloyal and faithless, as unreliable as a faulty bow. They angered him with their high places; they aroused his jealousy with their idols.

When God heard them, he was very angry; he rejected Israel completely. He abandoned the tabernacle of Shiloh, the tent he had set up among men. He sent the ark of his might into captivity, his splendor into the hands of the enemy. He gave his people over to the sword, he was very angry with his inheritance. Fire consumed their young men, and their maidens had no wedding songs; their priests were put to the sword, and their widows could not weep.

Then the Lord awoke as from sleep, as a man wakes from the stupor of wine. He beat back his enemies; he put them to everlasting shame. Then he rejected the tents of Joseph, he did not choose the tribe of Ephraim; but he chose the tribe of Judah, Mount Zion, which he loved. He built his sanctuary like the high mountains, like the earth that he established forever.

He chose David his servant and took him from the sheep pens, from tending the sheep he brought him to be the shepherd of his people Jacob, of Israel his inheritance. And David shepherded them with integrity of heart; with skillful hands he led them.

David was a shepherd.
Peter was a fisherman.
Paul, a tentmaker.
You call each of us, Lord,
from our daily tasks,
and make each of us
shepherds of the sheep in Your pasture,
fishers of men, and
builders of Your church.
You transform us by baptizing us
with fire from Your Spirit.

Your people will praise you forever

Help us, O God our Savior, for the glory of your name; deliver us and atone for our sins for your name's sake.

O God, the nations have invaded your inheritance; they have defiled your holy temple, they have reduced Jerusalem to rubble. They have given the dead bodies of your servants as food to the birds of the air, the flesh of your saints to the beasts of the earth. They have poured out blood like water all around Jerusalem, and there is no one to bury the dead. We are objects of reproach to our neighbors, of scorn and derision to those around us.

How long, O Lord? Will you be angry forever? How long will your jealousy burn like fire? Pour out your wrath on the nations that do not acknowledge you, on the kingdoms that do not call on your name; for they have devoured Jacob and destroyed his homeland. Do not hold against us the sins of the fathers; may your mercy come quickly to meet us, for we are in desperate need.

Help us, O God our Savior, for the glory of your name; deliver us and atone for our sins for your name's sake. Why should the nations say, "Where is their God?" Before our eyes, make known among the nations that you avenge the outpoured blood of your servants. May the groans of the prisoners come before you; by the strength of your arm preserve those condemned to die.

Pay back into the laps of our neighbors seven times the reproach they have hurled at you, O Lord. Then we your people, the sheep of your pasture, will praise you forever; from generation to generation we will recount your praise.

You chose Jerusalem, the holy city,
as the inheritance of Your people.
That is what makes her
unique and beautiful –
the centre of conflict too.
Jerusalem, you are lovely and majestic
as armies under banner.
We pray for your peace,
as we anticipate the Jerusalem from above!

Shine upon us

Restore us, O God Almighty; make your face shine upon us, that we may be saved.

Hear us, O Shepherd of Israel, you who lead Joseph like a flock; you who sit enthroned between the cherubim, shine forth before Ephraim, Benjamin and Manasseh. Awaken your might; come and save us.

Restore us, O God; make your face shine upon us, that we may be saved.

O Lord God Almighty, how long will your anger smolder against the prayers of your people?
You have fed them with the bread of tears; you have made them drink tears by the bowlful.
You have made us a source of contention to our neighbors, and our enemies mock us.

Restore us, O God Almighty; make your face shine upon us, that we may be saved.

Restore to us what the locust has eaten.
Restore upon us the shine from Your face.
You love the fellowship with Your people,
yet You must hide Your face,
suffering in such a way
only the almighty God can endure.
Fellowship with You comes in suffering.
Until the day You wipe the last tear away.

Revive us

*Return to us, O God Almighty! Look down from heaven and
see! Watch over this vine.
Let your hand rest on the man at your right hand, the son of
man you have raised up for yourself.*

You brought a vine out of Egypt; you drove out the nations
and planted it.
You cleared the ground for it, and it took root and filled the
land.
The mountains were covered with its shade, the mighty
cedars with its branches.
It sent out its boughs to the Sea, its shoots as far as the River.

Why have you broken down its walls so that all who pass by
pick its grapes?
Boars from the forest ravage it and the creatures of the field
feed on it.
Return to us, O God Almighty! Look down from heaven and
see! Watch over this vine, the root your right hand has
planted, the son you have raised up for yourself.

Your vine is cut down, it is burned with fire; at your rebuke
your people perish.
Let your hand rest on the man at your right hand, the son of
man you have raised up for yourself.
Then we will not turn away from you; revive us, and we will
call on your name.

Restore us, O Lord God Almighty; make your face shine
upon us, that we may be saved.

*Your kingdom starts out of a seed.
It is planted and tendered.
You give growth.
I thank You
for allowing me to be part of the vine,
and together with the others of Your planting,
able to experience the seasons of change:
the heartaches of autumn;
the dying of winter;
the triumphal renaissance of spring.
I am one of Your growing things.*

Sing for joy

am the Lord your God, who brought you up out of Egypt.
Open wide your mouth and I will fill it.

ing for joy to God our strength; shout aloud to the God of
acob! Begin the music, strike the tambourine, play the
melodious harp and lyre. Sound the ram's horn at the New
Moon, and when the moon is full, on the day of our Feast; this
a decree for Israel, an ordinance of the God of Jacob. He
stablished it as a statute for Joseph when he went out against
gypt, where we heard a language we did not understand.
le says, "I removed the burden from their shoulders; their
ands were set free from the basket. In your distress you
alled and I rescued you, I answered you out of a
hundercloud; I tested you at the waters of Meribah. *Selah.*
Hear, O my people, and I will warn you– if you would but
sten to me, O Israel! You shall have no foreign god among
ou; you shall not bow down to an alien god. I am the Lord
our God, who brought you up out of Egypt. Open wide your
nouth and I will fill it.
But my people would not listen to me; Israel would not
ubmit to me. So I gave them over to their stubborn hearts to
ollow their own devices.
If my people would but listen to me, if Israel would follow
y ways, how quickly would I subdue their enemies and turn
y hand against their foes! Those who hate the Lord would
ringe before him, and their punishment would last forever.
ut you would be fed with the finest of wheat; with honey
om the rock I would satisfy you."

hank You for calling me
nto the desert
here the noise of Egypt fades.
listen and hear Your assuring voice:
I will give you back your vineyards,
nake the valley of trouble into
door of hope.
here you will sing
s in the days of your youth."
praise You!
ou put a new song in my mouth;
art of a heavenly symphony.

Rescue the weak

They know nothing, they understand nothing. They walk about in darkness; all the foundations of the earth are shaken.

God presides in the great assembly; he gives judgment among the "gods": "How long will you defend the unjust and show partiality to the wicked? *Selah.*
Defend the cause of the weak and fatherless; maintain the rights of the poor and oppressed.
Rescue the weak and needy; deliver them from the hand of the wicked.

"They know nothing, they understand nothing. They walk about in darkness; all the foundations of the earth are shaken.

"I said, 'You are "gods"; you are all sons of the Most High.' But you will die like mere men; you will fall like every other ruler."

Rise up, O God, judge the earth, for all the nations are your inheritance.

I am heartbroken
as I consider the unrighteousness of man
and the violent offences against the weak.
God, show mercy on this earth!
Rescue those who are in need of You!
Deliver them
from the hand of the wicked.

Let them know you, God

Let them know that you, whose name is the Lord– that you alone are the Most High over all the earth.

O God, do not keep silent; be not quiet, O God, be not still.
See how your enemies are astir, how your foes rear their heads.
With cunning they conspire against your people; they plot against those you cherish.
"Come," they say, "let us destroy them as a nation, that the name of Israel be remembered no more."

With one mind they plot together; they form an alliance against you– the tents of Edom and the Ishmaelites, of Moab and the descendants of Hagar, Gebal, Ammon and Amalek, Philistia, with the people of Tyre.
Even Assyria has joined them to lend strength to the descendants of Lot. *Selah.*

Do to them as you did to Midian, as you did to Sisera and Jabin at the river Kishon, who perished at Endor and became like refuse on the ground.
Make their nobles like Oreb and Zeeb, all their princes like Zebah and Zalmunna, who said, "Let us take possesion of the pasturelands of God."

Make them like tumbleweed, O my God, like chaff before the wind.
As fire consumes the forest or a flame sets the mountains ablaze, so pursue them with your tempest and terrify them with your storm.
Cover their faces with shame so that men will seek your name, O Lord.

May they ever be ashamed and dismayed; may they perish in disgrace.
Let them know that you, whose name is the Lord– that you alone are the Most High over all the earth.

*My greatest fear is not suffering,
persecution, destruction, or pain.
What I really fear is
to end my days in futility,
barren for life in eternity.
Our temporal lives are the foundation
we lay for eternity.
Only love has eternal value.*

*Blessed are those
whose strength is in you, who have
set their hearts on pilgrimage. As they pass
through the Valley of Baca, they make it a place of
springs; the autumn rains also cover it with pools.
They go from strength to strength till
each appears before God
in Zion.*

Psalm 84

Place near your altar

Even the sparrow has found a home, and the swallow a nest
for herself, where she may have her young– a place near your
altar, O Lord Almighty, my King and my God.

How lovely is your dwelling place, O Lord Almighty!
My soul yearns, even faints for the courts of the Lord; my
heart and my flesh cry out for the living God.

Even the sparrow has found a home, and the swallow a nest
for herself, where she may have her young– a place near your
altar, O Lord Almighty, my King and my God.
Blessed are those who dwell in your house; they are ever
praising you. *Selah.*
Blessed are those whose strength is in you, who have set their
hearts on pilgrimage.
As they pass through the Valley of Baca, they make it a place
of springs; the autumn rains also cover it with pools.
They go from strength to strength till each appears before
God in Zion.

Hear my prayer, O Lord God Almighty; listen to me, O God
of Jacob. *Selah.*
Look upon our shield, O God; look with favor on your
anointed one.

Better is one day in your courts than a thousand elsewhere; I
would rather be a doorkeeper in the house of my God than
dwell in the tents of the wicked.
For the Lord God is a sun and shield; the Lord bestows favor
and honor; no good thing does he withhold from those whose
walk is blameless.

O Lord Almighty, blessed is the man who trusts in you.

As we left Egypt we were fugitives,
with the comforts of that land
still in our hearts.
But You brought us out;
through the desert of disillusion.
You made us a covenanted people,
and we gradually caught the vision
of the promised land.
From being fugitives we became pilgrims.

Surely his salvation is near

Faithfulness springs forth from the earth, and righteousness looks down from heaven.

You showed favor to your land, O Lord; you restored the fortunes of Jacob.
You forgave the iniquity of your people and covered all their sins. *Selah.*
You set aside all your wrath and turned from your fierce anger.

Restore us again, O God our Savior, and put away your displeasure toward us.
Will you be angry with us forever? Will you prolong your anger through all generations?
Will you not revive us again, that your people may rejoice in you?
Show us your unfailing love, O Lord, and grant us your salvation.

I will listen to what God the Lord will say; he promises peace to his people, his saints– but let them not return to folly.
Surely his salvation is near those who fear him, that his glory may dwell in our land.

Love and faithfulness meet together; righteousness and peace kiss each other. Faithfulness springs forth from the earth, and righteousness looks down from heaven.
The Lord will indeed give what is good, and our land will yield its harvest.
Righteousness goes before him and prepares the way for his steps.

From our folly we learned
the consequences of sin;
one sin reached out its dirty hand
to the next.
The final destiny: destruction and death.
Not so in Your kingdom,
where faithfulness follows love,
and righteousness kisses peace,
'til the land is ready for harvest.

Teach me your way

Hear my prayer, O Lord; listen to my cry for mercy.
In the day of my trouble I will call to you, for you will answer
me.

Hear, O Lord, and answer me, for I am poor and needy.
Guard my life, for I am devoted to you. You are my God;
save your servant who trusts in you.
Have mercy on me, O Lord, for I call to you all day long.
Bring joy to your servant, for to you, O Lord, I lift up my soul

You are kind and forgiving, O Lord, abounding in love to all
who call to you.
Hear my prayer, O Lord; listen to my cry for mercy.
In the day of my trouble I will call to you, for you will answer
me.
Among the gods there is none like you, O Lord; no deeds can
compare with yours.
All the nations you have made will come and worship before
you, O Lord; they will bring glory to your name.
For you are great and do marvelous deeds; you alone are
God.

Teach me your way, O Lord, and I will walk in your truth;
give me an undivided heart, that I may fear your name.
I will praise you, O Lord my God, with all my heart; I will
glorify your name forever.
For great is your love toward me; you have delivered my soul
from the depths of the grave.

The arrogant are attacking me, O God; a band of ruthless
men seeks my life– men without regard for you.
But you, O Lord, are a compassionate and gracious God,
slow to anger, abounding in love and faithfulness.
Turn to me and have mercy on me; grant your strength to
your servant and save the son of your maidservant.
Give me a sign of your goodness, that my enemies may see it
and be put to shame, for you, O Lord, have helped me and
comforted me.

As summer and winter alternate in my life
I will pray for a heart undivided.
When this world's facade seeks to capture me
I will pray to be kept on Your path.
Create in me now a clean heart
which reflects who You really are.
Watch over my coming and going
both now and for evermore.

*You led
your people like a flock
by the hand of Moses and
Aaron.*

Sing for joy to God our
strength; shout aloud to the God
of Jacob! Begin the music, strike the
tambourine, play the melodious harp and lyre.
Sound the ram's horn at the New Moon, and when the
moon is full, on the day of our Feast; this is a decree
for Israel, an ordinance of the God of Jacob. He
established it as a statute for Joseph
when he went out against Egypt,
where we heard a language we
did not understand.